Mark j. Wilson

How I amazingly steal my darling heart without spending money

Introduction

As a man, in the event that you 't give a sensible measure of cash for your lady, you might be viewed as a risk or somebody who has lost his privilege to be alluded to as a man.

This philosophy has eaten profound into the general public that it's not unexpected to see a person figuring out his butt just to put food on the table and take great consideration of his significant other and youngsters.

Be that as it may, assuming you are one who because of the current circumstance of things have lost the capacity to accommodate your lady, all trust isn't lost. There are different things you simply have to begin accomplishing other things to keep your lady cheerful. However, this doesn't mean you won't attempt to begin bringing in cash once more. It just takes that undying affection to see any individual who might stay with a man who can't deal with a person for quite a while.

Chapter 1

Despite the fact that cash is vital for the progress of each and every relationship, it is as yet workable for two lovebirds to live cheerfully without cash.

Utilize these tips to fulfill your lady without spending a dime:

1. Be true

Your million bucks can't get her joy. Ladies value men who are straightforward with them and nothing puts her off than an unscrupulous man. On the off chance that you could do without her outfit, cosmetics or a few propensities, just let her know as opposed to offering a constrained commendation.

2. Praises

We as a whole love praises however ladies specifically have a weakness for folks who praise them. Put forth the attempt to remind her how delightful she is and allowed her new looks never to slip by everyone's notice. Despite the fact that she definitely realizes she is pretty, it harms not to rehash it again and again assuming that fulfills her.

3. Make her supper

While most men could do without cooking, most ladies value a man who has the right stuff. Figure out how to cause her #1 food and let her lie on the love seat as you to get going in the kitchen every so often. Proposing to cook or do the dishes for her shows that you are a mindful and heartfelt fellow and that is the longing of each and every lady.

4. Get her blossoms

Go out to the nursery, pick a few blossoms and make her a delightful bouquet. Have the blossoms dropped at her work area at work with a little written by hand note with a sweet message. This will illuminate her day and you will stay in her viewpoints day in and day out.

5. Regard

Presently, I must underscore this as much as possible. In the male centric culture we are living in today, getting a man who truly regards a person for what her identity is all in all an undertaking. Regard her space, security, standards, choices and all that she does. Except if all she needs is your cash, no lady can stand a rude man in this age.

6. The easily overlooked details mean a ton

On the off chance that you stick around your young men throughout the entire year and she gripes, you will think she is getting frivolous. Yet, truly, those tiny things make the biggest difference to ladies. Stand by listening to her, show up for her, open the entryway for her value her endeavors.

Chapter 2

10 Unique Ways to Show Love Without Spending Money

a youthful couple wearing white lays in the grass

The best chance to show your affection for somebody is constantly, no matter what the season or your monetary circumstance. Whether you're celebrating familial love, heartfelt love, dispassionate love, or in the middle between, little demonstrations of friendship go quite far. Also, fortunately, there are a lot of ways you can show love without burning through cash on things like extravagant gifts and costly meals.

As the Beatles so appropriately put it, "can't get me love." Here are 10 methods for doing precisely that:

1. Make a photograph book or collection.

Print out your number one pictures of you and your cherished one and let your inventive energies stream. It's consistently perfect to open up a scrapbook or take a gander at a composition to keep a substantial hold of good recollections!

2. Or on the other hand go computerized, and alter a video.

Assuming you're to a greater degree a computerized imaginative, have a go at altering together a pleasant video that shows them you give it a second thought. Whether you need to star in the video or make everything about them depends on you. Free altering programming flourishes on the Internet, and in the event that you want an altering brief training, you can find instructional exercises online too.

3. Send them on a forager chase.

Compose puzzles or hints on sheets of paper and conceal them in different areas (maybe inside your home, or in the local you met in, or at your number one date spot). Your adored one should figure the response to each hint to see as the following one.

4. Curate an individual playlist for them.

Are there lots of melodies out there that help you to remember a unique somebody? Or on the other hand do you have any idea that individual so well that you can arrange an entire playlist of melodies they'll go off the deep end about? One way or the other, arranging a playlist on Spotify or Soundcloud is totally free and a magnificent method for showing them you give it a second thought.

5. Remain in for a comfortable film night.

Extra focuses on the off chance that you make a cool pad post. Goodness — and let them pick the movie(s)!

6. Offer up a help or favor (and really see everything through to completion).

Lift some weight off their shoulders by marking a thing off their daily agenda. To put in any amount of work, get up ahead of schedule and complete that errand so it's finished before they've even begun their day. You could likewise think about offering an expert help free of charge. Might you at any point plan a logo for their site or draft a financial plan for their impending venture? What could appear as though a commonplace expertise or undertaking for you could go quite far for another person!

7. Take them on a heartfelt climb.

Pick a recreation area and get going! You can never turn out badly with a stroll through lovely view.

8. Compose something pleasant for them.

It very well may be an affection letter, a haiku, an inside joke...just make a point to handwrite it. With a pen and paper. This is the ideal opportunity to possibly find some way to improve on those cursive abilities you haven't utilized since 5th grade.

9. Do an offhand photoshoot.

You don't require an extravagant camera for this. A cell phone will really do fine and dandy. Take a few imaginative photos of your cherished one and watch as their certainty skyrockets.

10. Dance together.

Turn up the music and let the great times roll. Moving is an incredible method for fashioning associations with individuals and to let them know you give it a second thought — without utilizing any words whatsoever.

Chapter 3

10 Costless Ways to Say "I Love You"

Prior to doling out tips on how you can communicate your adoration without spending anything, for what reason is it critical to make such an articulation in any case? At the point when you're seeing someone, ought to never underestimate your accomplice. Taking into account each second that you spend together as valuable is the most effective way to reinforce the bond that you have for one another. There's no assurance about how long the relationship will endure - even strong associations like relationships for the most part end up in a chaotic separation. So while you're still in that relationship, it is ideal to communicate your adoration for one another.

Presently, what are the main ten different ways for you to communicate your adoration without spending anything? Here is our main ten rundown:

1. Express your affection through little, regular motions

There are times when a stupendous motion appears to be empty or even unfilled, and it's the little, regular signals that count. You truly don't have to spend so much while communicating your affection to your life partner. Assuming your better half is griping that you're investing an excessive amount of energy at work, for instance, give a whole day to her.

Treat her to a heartfelt day at the recreation area where you can have an excursion without the children. Assuming she's consistently the one doing family tasks, tell her that you are eager to assist. Be liberal with your touch, kisses, embraces, and alternate ways of communicating your fondness. Do whatever easily falls into place. By giving your cherished one time and consideration, you don't for a moment even need to spend anything and that is as of now a method for communicating your adoration.

2. Treat your soul mate to a back rub

In the event that you have no clue about how to

give a back rub, go on the web and watch an educational video on YouTube. Search for how-to recordings for back rubs, foot rubs, a back knead or a full body rub. Before you nod off, set the state of mind in the room by lighting scented candles or diminishing the lights, and playing music.

Use body salve or oil, then, at that point, request that your accomplice rests on the bed. A thirty moment to one-hour full body rub, a back rub or even a basic foot rub is a great treat to give your accomplice, which likewise serves as a method for communicating your adoration. In the event that you see that your companion had an unrelenting workday, a foot rub, a speedy back knead or a head back rub will likewise do ponders.

3. Be available to your darling no matter what for one day

Good times ought to continuously be consolidated seeing someone, what better way is there for you to both have some good times than alternating being available to one another no matter what? Suppose that you are approaching your commemoration and you are searching for ways of flavoring things up in the room. For the very first moment, you can be available to your darling no matter what for a whole day.

You need to do whatever your accomplice orders - be it in or out of the room. For day two, it will be your move and you can have a good time outshining your accomplice's orders. The help can be just about as basic as serving breakfast in bed, or as wicked as touching your accomplice's body in the shower. Utilize your creative mind and you will track down a lot of ways of having a great time while reinforcing your personal bond simultaneously.

4. Deal with his/her stomach

You've proactively heard the banality that the way to a man's heart is through his stomach. On the off chance that you're a man, you can constantly follow a similar mantra and cook for your soul mate. Serve her morning meal in bed, or free your better half from errands and cook a decent supper for her.

The dishes don't for a moment even must be intricate on the off chance that you truly have no cooking abilities. Search for straightforward recipes online that you can follow. Regardless of whether the dishes end up being as delectable, it's the work behind the signal that your accomplice will certainly appreciate.

5. Make something carefully assembled

In the event that you're great at drawing, why not make a high quality card with a sweet note for your accomplice? Regardless of whether there's no exceptional event, the person will most likely value the immediacy of the signal. Assuming you have abilities at weaving, sewing or stitching, make something hand tailored for your better half.

Regardless of whether a scarf just expense you the cost of one roll of yarn, it's the work behind the sewing and the time that you spent completing the job which will communicate your affection without words.

6. Accomplish something unconstrained or fun together

When did that you and your accomplice last accomplish something fun and unconstrained together? In the event that it's been ages since you went out for a walk, put on your running outfit and work out together. Investigate the neighborhood plant life in your space and go out for a walk. Pack several sandwiches and drinks in your knapsack and shock your collaborate with an unconstrained excursion after a climb.

Look at the schedule of exercises in your space where you can look at rancher's business sectors, entertainments parks or craftsmanship displays together. To set aside cash, consider the time that you can get in for nothing or with limited extra charges.

7. Give your accomplice praises

When did that you last offer your accomplice a commendation? While your better half is sprucing up for work, give him an embrace from behind and let him know how attractive you think he looks. Spouses ought to continuously give their wives praises. In addition to the fact that this is an extraordinary method for supporting her confidence, but at the same time it's a great method for communicating your affection.

The more unconstrained and genuine the commendation is, the better. You might make things one stride further by astounding your cherished one with a note embedded at his portfolio or inside her sack with a charming or wicked commendation in it.

8. Award a wish

Assuming it's your better half's birthday and you have no financial plan for a sumptuous present, make a handcrafted coupon demonstrating that you can act as your accomplice's genie for a day - and award one wish. It very well may be a sexual place that you realize your accomplice has for a long time needed to attempt. It very well may be simply going through a whole day together without both of you minding your cell phone or PC.

It very well may be a fast escape at a lodge in the timberland, where you can essentially appreciate each other's conversation. In this quick moving world, what's truly ailing in connections is the time that the couple really enjoy with one another. Regardless of whether you are snuggling together, your considerations may be on a little screen rather than at one another. Conceding a wish is something straightforward that you can accomplish for one another which fills in as an effective method for communicating your adoration, without spending anything.

9. Sort out a game night with your accomplice's companions

Assuming that you realize that it's been ages since your beau has invested energy with his nearest fellow companions, shock him by putting together a game night at your place. Let your sweetheart know that you simply need to go through a calm night together, however watchfully reach out to the young men and let them know that you are coordinating a game evening.

Set up a region in the house where they can get

together and request that the folks bring alcohol, cigarettes, and munchies. You should simply ensure that there's a room that they can use as a gaming region - which you can stock with decks of cards that they can use for poker night. He will clearly be shocked and moved by the signal.

10. Be additional sweet

At last, being additional sweet to your soul mate is most likely the best yet most affordable way for you to communicate your affection. Beside giving your accomplice praises, be extra gushy. On the off chance that you're awkward with public showcases of friendship, shock your accomplice by giving him a little kiss on the lips once you see each other out in the city. At home, be liberal with your touch, much love. Be unconstrained, unwind, and simply appreciate each other's conversation.

Chapter 4

Customarily men think the main things that satisfy a young lady is purchasing shoes, costly presents, and extravagant cafés. While those things are great, a gift for lady can't supplant these basic moves toward satisfying a lady. Bliss is the strong groundwork a marriage or relationship is based on. In this way, guaranteeing your companion or accomplice is blissful ought to be a main concern for anybody dating, wedded or in a relationship. A small amount sentiment can make a remarkable difference to make a young lady cheerful and it should frequently be sans possible or exceptionally modest.

Offer commendations Women need to feel pretty. Ladies need to feel like they are the most appealing individual in the room, in any event, when they first creep up in the first part of the day. They likewise love to be told when something they do satisfies their man. A basic, "You look pretty today." or, "That was an extraordinary supper. Did you make it in an unexpected way?" Can go quite far to fulfill a young lady. Basic commendations let ladies know that you notice and you give it a second thought.

Listen-This implies simply tune in. Men are "fix-it" types and consistently attempt to think of arrangements. More often than not, ladies don't need an answer. They simply need to vent. In the event that a lady doesn't request an answer, in all probability she simply needs to have the option to move it out into the open and track down a thoughtful ear. It can fulfill a young lady just to have somebody that she can communicate her sentiments to and realize that individual is truly tuning in.

Contact her-This is a very surprising step for ladies than it is for men. Ladies very much prefer to be contacted essentially to be contacted. Something as straightforward as running your give over her back or hauling the hair out of her eyes shows a lady that you love her. Only one out of every odd touch needs to have sexual undertones. Truth be told, ladies very much want the contacts that are essentially a demonstration of fondness. If you have any desire to fulfill a young lady, this is a significant stage to recollect.

Be genuine. Ladies can figure out whether you are just professing to tune in or praises are constrained. Regardless of what you do or say, ensure that it is in the sincerest structure. Ladies would rather not hear, "You look pretty today," in the event that it comes out seeming like you read it off a sign card

6 hints to fulfill a lady without cash

Be earnest. Your million bucks can't get her bliss.

...

Praises. We as a whole love praises yet ladies specifically have a weakness for folks who praise them. ...

Make her supper. ...

Get her blossoms. ...

Regard. ...

The easily overlooked details mean a ton.

Likewise What could I at any point do with my better half with no cash? Attempt these 10 things when you have NO cash:

Compose letters. Composing a letter is a wonderful approach to speaking with anyone. ...

Get imaginative with food. ...

Make gifts together. ...

Volunteer. ...

Snooze longer. ...

Utilize Netflix. ...

Explore different avenues regarding your hairdos. ...

Spa day at home.

Could a lady at any point cherish you without cash? Your adoration can't survive without cash

Furthermore, it is basically impossible that you will do these without spending. At the point when the activity of cash in connections and relationships is discussed nowadays, a great deal of consideration is paid on ladies and how they need to contribute all the more consistently and burn through cash on men, as well.

Indistinguishably How would I keep a relationship with no cash? Here are a few different ways that will assist you with scoring focuses even without spending any additional cash.

Be 100 percent present when you're together. There will constantly be more work. ...

Depict all that you do together as exceptional, regardless of how basic. ...

Continuously understand what free stuff could be done beyond the home.

Related Contents [show]

How might I draw in a young lady?

Get to know her.

Regard her thoughts, her perspectives, and her convictions. Young ladies like it when you deal with them like individuals. In the event that you believe young ladies should think that you are alluring, regarding them as individuals is an extraordinary spot to begin. For instance, get some information about her #1 side interest, and afterward ask her how she got into that leisure activity.

How would I prevail upon her? The following are

10 methods for prevailing upon a young lady:

Be compatible. Seek after her without the tension. ...

Be a man of his word. Young ladies would rather not be dealt with like a sovereign, yet they would like to be dealt with like a princess. ...

Be free. ...

Be inventive. ...

Be purposeful. ...

Praise her before others. ...

Be mindful. ...

Be defensive.

likewise What compel a young lady succumb to you? Step by step instructions to Make a Girl Fall For You: 20 Simple Strategies

Work on yourself and have your own life. ...

Be hopeful. ...

Make a big difference for the discussion. ...

Regard her as an equivalent. ...

Be her companion and make it fun. ...

Be everything except tenacious. ...

Go slowly - things will fall set up. ...

Try not to make yourself excessively accessible.

How do u make a young lady miss u?

Which word intrigue a young lady?

The main tip when you need to intrigue young ladies with words is to convey a feeling of predominance while being heartfelt.

Jargon to dazzle your better half or date.

Alluring. Alluring means appealing. ...

Wondrous. ...

Shocking. ...

Rich. ...

Stunning. ...

Bewitching. ...

Striking.

How can you say whether a young lady loves you? Signs a Girl Likes You

Her loved ones are familiar you. ...

She reschedules a date she can't make. ...

She really tries to proceed with the discussion. ...

She praises you and attempts to encourage you. ...

She's plainly apprehensive around you. ...

Her non-verbal communication is welcoming. ...

She recalls things you tell her.

What things do young ladies jump at the chance to hear?

30 Things Women Always Want to Hear

"You Know What I Love About You?" Followed by

something exceptionally definite. ...

"You're Right." ...

"You Look Amazing." ...

"We're In This Together." ...

"The previous evening Was Incredible." ...

"To Talk, I'm Here." ...

"What's The Most Meaningful Experience You've Ever Had?" ...

"No, You Don't Look Fat."

How might I make a young lady fall head over heels for me through talking? 21 Ways To Impress A Girl In Chat Conversation

Be the one to constantly begin the visit discussion. ...

Show restraint toward her in any event, when she doesn't focus on you. ...

Give her the feeling that you're earnest with her. ...

Try not to come down on her to discuss herself.

...

Put forth attempts to be aware of her at her own speed.

How might I be heartfelt to my sweetheart?

Underline her character characteristics – notice how innovative or unconstrained she is and the amount you respect it. Express appreciation for her everyday activities. Show her that you notice she required some investment to do her hair in another manner or attempted to assemble another look with her garments. Tell her how she affects you.

How might I make my better half wild about me?

Cause her to feel extraordinary.

On the off chance that you believe a young lady should go off the deep end for you, you need to cause her to feel extraordinary by really finding opportunity to perceive her as a special person. Tell her, "dislike different young ladies... " or "You're so unique in relation to your companions... " and make her see that she truly stands apart to you.

How might I make my better half obsessed with me once more? 10 Ways to Make Her Fall in Love With You All Over Again

Pay attention to Her. ...

Praise Her Looks. ...

Try not to Shy Away from Chivalry. ...

Support Her Decisions. ...

Tell Her How Much You Love Her. ...

Offer Her Consideration. ...

Sustain the Love between You. ...

Looking Good.

How might I make her need me once more? Tell her how you feel.

Be explicit. Show her how you've really tried to change as opposed to making void commitments.

Give her time. In the event that she's hesitant from the outset, don't blow up or disheartened. Recollect that regardless of whether she need you back, she actually needs to safeguard her heart.

How would I make my better half cry?

101 Sweet Things To Say To Your Girlfriend To Make Her Cry

You convince me to get up in the first part of the day.

Your voice advises me that there's bliss on the planet.

I was continuously searching for joy and I have tracked down it in us.

Prevent the world from turning since I need to get off with you.

How would I fulfill my sweetheart over text? Step by step instructions to Make a Girl Happy over Text

1 Lead in with something that will intrigue her.

2 Ask her for a proposal.

3 Give her a commendation.

4 Tell her that something helped you to remember her.

5 Make her grin with something adorable or interesting.

6 Ask her inquiries concerning herself.

7 Let her know you're there for her.

How would I sentiment my sweetheart in message?

Heartfelt Text Message Ideas for Her and Him.

...

Heartfelt Good Night Messages

Come to my fantasies if possible. ...

This evening I'll nod off with you in my heart.

You will be the final thing I consider before I

tumble to rest and first thing to recall when I awaken.

Regular I enjoy with you is the new greatest day of my life.

What inquiries to pose to your better half to check whether she cherishes you? 20 Questions to Ask Your Girlfriend

How's something you'd very much want to respond this month?

How might I improve your life today?

What might you like our common objectives to be this year?

In what ways do you feel cherished by me?

What are the things I do that you appreciate?

What are the things I do that bother you?

What inquiries to pose to a young lady to be aware on the off chance that she cherishes you?

Thus, here is a rundown of adoration inquiries to pose to a young lady:

What is the most heartfelt excursion you fantasy about going on?

Which tune rings a bell and heart, while you think about me?

How is the best thing you about me?

What is the best genuine romance story you have heard?

When did you first fall head over heels for me?

How can you say whether your better half doesn't cherish you? In the event that she continually concocts pardons not to invest energy with you, there's a decent opportunity she doesn't cherish you any longer. What's more, an amazing opportunity she's focusing on another person over you. You could believe on the off chance that she texts you continually, she's showing she's intrigued.

What could a young lady at any point like in a person?

Certainty. Certainty is likely the main thing that young ladies search for in young men. ...

Great Grooming. If a person has any desire to stand out, he ought to keep essential preparing guidelines, for example, showering, wearing antiperspirant, and wearing clean garments. ...

Better than average of Humor. ...

Simple to Talk to. ...

Actual Attraction. ...

Regard.

What are the three words to dazzle a young lady? In only three straightforward words, you can communicate your affections for your crush, your better half or your significant other.

...

Investigate this rundown of 18 #ThreeWordsSheWantsToHear underneath:

I love you. ...

You're the one. ...

Simply kiss me! ...

Limitless hot pizza... ...

You're the G.O.A.T. ...

I miss you. ...

Gather your packs!

What do young ladies want to be aware of young men?

THINGS GIRLS WANT TO KNOW ABOUT GUYS| My Boyfriend's Perspective

Why folks are not straight forward in the event that they like me or not? ...

What folks truly search in a relationship? ...

What is one quality folks love in a young lady? ...

Your thought process could be the ideal first date? ...

What are 3 things young ladies do that folks loathe?

How might I talk in affection?

Let your accomplice know what you like.

Praise their character. Say, "I love conversing with you. You generally make me laugh uncontrollably."

Praise their looks. Say, "I can't quit pondering your eyes. Miss you."

Praise their abilities. Say, "You kiss me so indeed, it's making me insane that I can't do it at the present time."

How might I converse with my better half without exhausting? Try not to exhaust! Be open, defenseless, and fair. Answer questions and ask them back when you're finished answering. Try not to propose single word replies, which will generally end discussions in their tracks.

What are the points to converse with a young lady?

20 Topics To Talk About With A Girl

Her day. Try not to simply ask a fundamental 'how are you? ...

Likes. Examining likes is a basic easy decision method for getting to realize anybody better, as how an individual appreciates doing their time, shows a major piece of their personality. ...

Hates. ...

Side interests. ...

Objectives. ...

Accomplishments. ...

Family. ...

Companions.

Chapter 5

Love Or Money: What's More Important To You And Why?

Love is perhaps of the best inspiration that an individual can have throughout everyday life. Having the option to encounter love is vital when you need to be content. However, there are individuals who aren't as worried about affection as others. Certain individuals are significantly more worried about bringing in cash and they appear to zero in on monetary accomplishment to the detriment of their affection lives. Certain individuals just search for men and cash; it simply relies upon what you esteem in affection and assuming that you at any point ask yourself is love enough?

Deciding if love or cash is overwhelmingly significant in your life appears to be legit. You should have the option to focus on things in your day to day existence. To be basically as cheerful as could really be expected, then, at that point, you need to ponder whether what you're doing will lead you down the right street. Pause for a minute to look at whether you ought to be more centered around tracking down adoration or bringing in cash. It could assist you with get-together your own contemplations regarding this situation so you can all the more likely center your own life objectives.

Why Is It Important to Worry About Money?

You likely know why stressing over money is significant. Cash is a need in this world. You should have the option to bring in a specific measure of cash just to have the option to scrape by. On the off chance that you bring in sufficient cash to be agreeable, you might actually begin purchasing additional things to build your way of life.

Having the option to purchase things truly will help you have a positive outlook on yourself. You can buy a pleasant new house, a decent vehicle, and numerous things that cause you to feel like your diligent effort has been beneficial. Zeroing in on your vocation has a reason and you will be compensated for having the option to keep on progressing up the profession stepping stool. However, this doesn't imply that cash is a higher priority than adoration.

The Importance Of Love

Love is something that you shouldn't need to live without in light of the significance of adoration and fondness. The vast majority have friends and family that they care about beyond a doubt. Regardless of whether you have a better half, you probably have companions or family that adoration you. Having individuals who love you assists you with encountering the genuine delights of life, and it's especially beneficial to find somebody that you can impart a heartfelt love association with.

In the event that you can find a darling then you will actually want to have somebody that you can impart your life to on an exceptionally profound level. Being fortified with somebody like this truly has an effect with regards to your general joy.

Having somebody who can partake in your satisfaction makes things that vastly improved. It's additionally perfect to have somebody that you can depend on during difficult stretches and it makes it simpler to overcome wild timeframes.

Being infatuated can cause you to feel like the world is that a lot more splendid. A wide range of adoration are vital and ought to be valued. Companionship has incredible worth and family ties are likewise something that you'll constantly hold near your heart. Heartfelt love is just something that can cause you to feel more complete personally.

Certain individuals end up abandoning tracking down adoration because of having awful encounters before. Love is somewhat of a situation with two sides along these lines. It can cause you to feel the most noteworthy of highs when things are going perfectly. It likewise can possibly lay you low when a relationship reaches a conclusion. It's not unexpected vital that you track down the fortitude to cherish again when you've encountered a misfortune like this. Love creates the world a superior spot and it can truly work on your personal satisfaction when you can track down an adoration that endures.

It Is Key to Find A Balance

Finding an equilibrium in your life will be the way to being genuinely blissful. You can't zero in on affection to the detriment of your vocation. There is an old term that says, "Love doesn't take care of the bills." This is valid generally and you really do have to ponder attempting to bring in sufficient cash so you can live serenely. Notwithstanding, seeking after monetary accomplishment to the detriment of your own happiness isn't solid.

In the event that you can figure out how to offset your profession objectives with your relationship objectives, then, at that point, things will be vastly improved. You'll have the option to appreciate all that adoration can bring into your life while as yet having the option to feel pleased with your profession achievement. Having the right degree of monetary achievement will make it conceivable to seek after beginning a family too. You should have the option to deal with your family in the event that you will have kids and attempt to experience anything that your vision of an ideal existence with your accomplice is.

Give your all to find a profession way that gives you sufficient opportunity to zero in on the things that you love. You should have the option to invest energy with your better half, and you additionally need to possess energy for the other notable individuals in your day to day existence. Working constantly is essentially not going to be solid. A more adjusted presence will assist you with making every second count.

Making some sort of timetable for yourself could end up aiding you out, as well. On the off chance that you're somewhat of an obsessive worker, as it were, you could have to set a few principles, similar to no noting work messages after supper or checking your cell phone while you're investing energy with your better half. Work and monetary achievement ought to expand your joy when you can figure out how to invest sufficient energy with your friends and family.

Recall That Money Can't Buy Love

You ought to constantly attempt to recollect that the familiar saying of "cash can't purchase love" is quite obvious. Individuals could end up rushing to you in the event that you become rich, however it could not necessarily be on the grounds that they genuinely love you. Cash isn't something going to have the option to comfort you while you're feeling down genuinely. It probably won't be as fulfilling without somebody to impart your life to.

People are social animals naturally and they want love. It's generally expected to need to be cherished however you can't get the affection that you're looking for essentially by making a lot of cash. Monetary achievement is honorable, and it's even vital to attempt to be monetarily secure. It's only pivotal to have the option to separate between the significance of cash and the genuine worth of affection.

On the off chance that you need to pick either cash and love, many individuals would propose that you pick love. A definitive decision is truly dependent upon you. You need to ponder what means a lot to you throughout everyday life. Assuming bringing in cash is really what you're most enthusiastic about throughout everyday life, then that is for you to choose.

Treatment Can Help Those Who Have Love Problems

You wouldn't believe the number of individuals that need to look for help for issues connected with adoration. Love is something that can make sensations of bitterness or withdrawal while it's absent from your life. In the event that you've been investing an excess of energy zeroing in on propelling your vocation, and it has cost you a portion of your satisfaction, then make sure to connect and get treatment. Advisors can assist you with managing nervousness and misery issues actually.

A gifted specialist is likewise going to have the option to assist you with assessing what is happening. It isn't continuously going to be straightforward your own sentiments. You could have to talk things over with an expert to truly figure out what is happening in your mind. Whatever you need to deal with, treatment can help. On the off chance that you believe treatment should be just about as advantageous as could really be expected, you might wish to pursue online treatment.

For instance, studies have shown that web-based treatment is valuable for individuals who need to address complex sentiments In a review distributed in the Journal of Medical Internet Research, the viability of online treatment while treating those with wretchedness and nervousness was noticed. Specialists explicitly used web-based mental conduct treatment (CBT), which is intended to assist members with supplanting meddling, pessimistic considerations that can prompt bothersome ways of behaving and feelings. The review inferred that internet based treatment assists with working with critical positive outcomes. Peruse beneath for certain audits of Better Help instructors, from individuals encountering comparative issues.

www.ingramcontent.com/pod-product-compliance
Lightning Source LLC
LaVergne TN
LVHW020524160826
845677LV00015B/3888

* 9 7 9 8 8 4 7 6 0 2 4 0 2 *